NO HIDING PLACE

TRACEY HERD

No Hiding Place

BLOODAXE BOOKS

ISBN: 1 85224 381 3

First published 1996 by
Bloodaxe Books Ltd,
P.O. Box 1SN,
Newcastle upon Tyne NE99 1SN.

Bloodaxe Books Ltd acknowledges
the financial assistance of Northern Arts.

Cover printing by J. Thomson Colour Printers Ltd, Glasgow.

Printed in Great Britain by
Cromwell Press Ltd, Broughton Gifford, Melksham, Wiltshire.

for Dave

Acknowledgements

Acknowledgements are due to the editors of the following publications in which some of these poems, or earlier versions of them, first appeared: *Eric*, *Gairfish (Duende: A Dundee Anthology*, 1991), *The Gregory Anthology 1991-1993* (Sinclair-Stevenson, 1993), *New Women Poets* (Bloodaxe Books, 1990), *Verse* and *Writing Women*.

I would like to thank the Society of Authors for an Eric Gregory Award in 1993 and the Scottish Arts Council for a Writer's Bursary in 1995.

Contents

The Survivors

I came at night to the dark house
where the father had taken the fuse
from the fuse-box and killed the lights.

I came at night when the weepy mother sat
doll-like in the front room, cross-legged on the carpet,
hands stinging from smacking the brats,

listening to crackly recordings of Glenn Miller,
her heels drumming on the well-worn floor:
the plane crash had wiped her mind out.

The thumb-sized father climbed the stairs
with a candle, searching for survivors.

The Bathing Girls

Lighting her thin French cigarette
with a flaring match, flinging her head
back to exhale her looping signature
in smoke, she plucked April's *Vogue*
from her smart red corduroy satchel.

She wet her thumb and peeled
the cover back. Sunlight fell
on an interior pungent and dazzling
as freshly painted walls. I breathed
deeply and took the plunge.

Six bathing girls in strapless suits
linked arms and ran out from a cerulean
ocean, their ankles fluted columns
tilting through the waves.
I hugged my school books close

not wanting to see how my friend's sweater
clung to her tiny breasts, but unable
to take my eyes from her slicked red mouth.
I wanted to lean forward and kiss her.
In those days, anything seemed possible.

A-Z

I open up an *A-Z* of London,
bending the covers tightly back.
Welts rise along its spine.
Page seventy-five is where I'm headed.
I reach for my watch and pen.
I will take the Underground
to Earl's Court and from there
enjoy a brisk walk to my destination.
I will savour the sinking afternoon sun
and the attendant October chills,
exhaust fumes and the glittering flow
of cars. I may stop at a jewellers
along the way and peer through the glass
at sapphires, diamonds, plain gold bands.
I will close my eyes and picture
the most expensive item on her slender finger.
I will probably arrive there
just as she returns from work –
I know she sometimes leaves
her back door off the latch.
I want it to be a surprise
so I'll wait till she's taken off her coat,
switched the television on
and patted cushions into place.
By then it will be dark. The moon
will be full, the stars respectful
in their supporting roles.
I finger the satin lining of the box.

The Snow Storm

She appeared to me twice in one evening
like the moon spreading across a snow-field
blue and freezing, electric at its edges.
Her smile was not human. Something
of her had already left the room, leaving only
her delicate frame to slip silently
out the back way while the tea-time dishes
were being cleared and the nurses' backs were turned.

She made it unnoticed to the laundry-room,
her bare feet leaving no tracks
in the snowy corridors. The windows
were giant sheets of black ice
where cars and bikes skidded off
into the whiteout. Every streetlight
had been extinguished by the storm.
The moon flickered off and on.

Soap Queen

A cold night in November: I blew on my hands.
The radiator pipes stayed tight-lipped.
'Put on more jumpers,' my mother told me,
'we're not heating the house up just for you.'

Downstairs the television set cranked out
bullets, smiles, rows of glittering, orange-
cheeked dancing girls. My parents posed
side by side on the settee, my mother

folding up her housecoat to expose
her left leg from thigh to feather slipper.
I smelled Cyclax and cheap Boots talcum powder.
One night in three, I sat in a lukewarm bath

and chewed up my legs with a blunt razor,
shouting if father creaked too near to the door.
Mother wandered in and out
with her unbuttoned dressing gown

flashing the obligatory three-quarters of a leg
and her flat chest, as white and smooth
as soap. Sometimes she'd throw open
the window, tut-tutting at the steam

and I'd shiver at the sudden inrush of air,
draw my bleeding knees up to my chin.

The Pink Rose Rings

She remembered seeing the underpass up ahead
and thinking how cool it would be when they slipped
into its shade. That was mere seconds before his hands
flew to the black hole in his throat. She turned
then, dazzled, the sun seeming to explode
beside her in the car. She remembered
the intricate pink rose rings in his skull, vivid
as the flowers that lay beside them on the seat,
and cradling his head, bewildered by the riot
of colour, wilting a little in the unseasonable heat.

Sir Ivor

Even those watching
the race repeated will swear every time
that he's beaten. He *must*
have sprouted wings between
the furlong pole and home. Press
your nose up against the screen
till the light blurs
on an imperceptible shifting
of gears, a heavenly guidance:
poor Connaught, only second
when you knew you'd won, your
big white face vanishing
like a ghost from the winner's enclosure
as Sir Ivor stepped through you.

In the Glassy Stream

Ophelia, relaxed and tearless
after her dazzling nonsense
is floating face-up in the water.

The flowers sprouted from her mouth
and snaked through her fingers.
Above all else, she was practical

and self-effacing, a modest girl
who gathered the crow flowers and the nettles
for her own funeral as all around her the plot unravelled.

Her broken judgement served her well.
The sun is smudging her features:
her skirts and her hair are fanned out like the willow.

Words of Love

Sex is carnage, he said
poised above her like a knife.

I love your mouth, he said,
or what's left of it.

I don't believe in love
or God, she said
and immediately regretted it.

I have a theory, he said,
about life, death, God; life
being a train journey
of divinely ordained length.
We step on, we step off.

Your arse and cunt look like
a butcher's shop, he said
rubbing his fingers along her bloody crack.

Girl Detective

My father is a famous lawyer.
He adores me. There is no mother
to get in the way. She died when I was three,
leaving the plump, friendly housekeeper
who is concerned for me.
I have been titian-haired and delicately pretty
for three-quarters of a century.
I have an eye for a mystery.

I am often praised for my cool head,
despite having been drugged,
gagged, bound by all manner of villains.
I have tripped over tree roots, fallen
down stairs. I have seen stars,
choked on cloths soaked in chloroform.
It's enough to make a girl scream
but I prefer the cold stare and the stinging retort.

No villain has ever gotten the better of me.
Not one. They are, without exception,
swarthy and unattractive, probably foreign.
The women are crueller than the men
but they break down more easily in the end.
They talk in stage whispers, in a special code.
They have raised indiscretion to an art,
turning up in rest-rooms and at gas-stations,
passing notes and dropping handy clues.
The Chief says be at H.Q. by three.

Wherever I'm headed, they'll be.
It's uncanny: Montreal, New York, the Adirondacks
or overseas. I have travelled
a pale, whimsical version of the world
on a limitless stream of dollars.
I catch my villain and hand him over.
He is scrubbed from the face of the earth forever.
There will be plenty of others.
I shut my front door on the world.

Once, between cases, frozen in time,
I dreamed I died and was buried
in a simple ceremony
on the outskirts of River Heights.
They laid me down next to my mother's body.
After the mourners had gone
I simply climbed, Houdini that I am,
out of the hole in the ground
back into the arms of my beloved father.
I kissed his face, then turned mine
into the cold October sun. It was evening.
We linked arms and walked quietly home.

The Siege

The twilight is a cathedral: a hymn
to summer thumps against the rafters
of the sky. The voices of the congregation
are cold and clear as holy water.

The heart is a walled city, thriving
but assailable. Only I know my way
here, each street's history, naming
them for kings and queens. Cramped alleys

bear the names of saints, and the tapestries
hanging in the fine museum
show soldiers under a smoking sky,
heretics dragged from secret rooms.

Their souls were purged and returned to God.
This is another century: my heart is peaceful.
I have unpicked the scarlet and gold threads
of their agony. Their blistered hands embroider angels.

Stallion Graveyard, Kentucky

The grass is lush but well tended.
The graves are ornaments
backlit to perfection by the sun.

Nashua, striking in bronze,
turns his handsome head
to his Negro stable-boy
in a savage gesture of love.

This is Bluegrass Country
and here lie the noble dead of Kentucky.
Some fell in their lovely prime
wrestled by lightning to the ground.
Others grew fat and almost tame.

On the first Saturday in May, at dawn,
the horsemen come to Churchill Downs.
The field is bloodlit viridian: guns
and cannon tear the silks of summer.
A fallen army stirs.
Their names are battle cries:
Cavalcade, Whirlaway, Gallahadion,
Count Fleet, Assault, Dark Star,
Dust Commander.

Rosery

He will reward her for her devotions;
not for the hours spent kneeling in prayer,
but rather the afternoons on the parched back green
with watering-can and pruning-shears,

the front door bolted firmly against all-comers
and the telephone, leaving the dear, distant
relatives to carry on their uncivil war:
four fading English roses ranged against

the martyred son who drags his home-made cross
up and down the garden path, while his unlovely wife
plays a one-woman Greek chorus
lamenting the burdens of his life.

Perhaps she worried away at the soil
to uncover the tablet of stone
that would miraculously explain it all,
until hot and discouraged she laid down

her tools and sprinkled rose-water
over her feet and hands, a helpless gesture
before the grandchildren piled out of the car
and stormed the sacred grove. These darling little flowers

bearing gifts and bearing down,
crushing herbs and petals in their careless flight
as they raced to be the one to turn
the sprinkler on the dozing cat.

May God gift you a blooming rosery
with neat borders, lush cropped lawn,
trellises, a sheer sky-wall, no means of entry
not even for saints, animals or small children.

The Tapestry

The Prince lies motionless
in the grass. His riderless horse
distractedly crops his flesh:
tiny pearls of bone on its shoulders
sprout into wings.

Inside the Great Hall,
meat is torn from bone
and ornate goblets crash together.
The vaulted ceilings split,
fault-lines sprinting
over every stone. Outside,
an orchestra of thunder rolls through
its dislocated repertoire.

The tapestry foretold it all,
that or the stars. They saw
the princess running from the tower
to crack the golden strands of hair
from her Prince's fist,
the straws he clutched at
as he fell backwards into air.

She mounts the horse and together
they gallop up the spiral stairs
that rise beyond the ruined tower,
stepping off into a forest of stars.

Missing

By Monday morning it seems certain
that the chill of his absence
will be permanent.

This is his map
spread out on the counter-top,
imagine where he wandered

dizzy and frozen
along the death-route.
An invisible X marks the spot.

Coronach

The skylark's melody is sealed in ice:
a coronach as blue as the winter
sky. The moon wobbles over the rock face,
throwing into high relief the climber
in a gully below the glittering maze.

He is a brilliant figure in this frieze.
His genius walked him into space
and left him to find a foothold there.
The moon is sheer ice or a cracked watch-face
that swings on its fragile chain of stars.

Night is falling at its own modest pace.

The Dinner Party

The curtains hang in strips
of seaweed green, lashing out
at wind and rain.
The sea shuffles closer.

A wine-glass explodes in my hand;
wine sprays the tablecloth like a butterfly
frenetically printing its wings
on a windshield.

Outside, the water and the sky
are the haphazard results
of a child with no patience
and three colours left on his palette.

The other guests move in and out
of focus like drowning men.
I am in over my head,
going down for the third time.

Our hostess clutches
an imaginary rail for balance
as she moves forward
carrying platters of black, stinking meat.

Paris in the Spring

Mother is in Paris for the spring collections.
She flies there and back within the hour.
In the kitchen, Father impatiently shakes out
his paper, scanning the business pages.
Outside the clouds air their linens
briskly; mother's laundry billows
into flower; the roses sway
in April's warm pastels.

Faces ring the catwalk. She is their centre.
Flashbulbs almost break her concentration
but she focuses ahead on a point the size of a coin
and spins triumphantly on one spike-heel.
Her mind winds the spool back thirty years
to a beach in Spain where a girl poses stiffly
in a swimsuit of dark green, her arms
stapled to her sides. She struggles
to free them, jumping back as she slops tea
over the mug's rim. Father tuts
and lays aside his paper.
Her head is in the clouds again.

The Gatecrashers

(for Isobel and John)

I step out onto the porch to clear my head.
The flagstones shift without warning
and the landscape itself is fluid:
the elegant sweep of the gravel drive,
then the garden, then the steep drop to the village
and its swarm of lights. Night
blacks out the fields and hedges,
three miles of arable land.
If I were to make my way down the lawn
and step over the low wall
I would be in free fall, shadowing the pilot
who bailed out over here during the war
somersaulting wildly
down the unravelling ladder of stars.
In the nearest field I rode the pony,
the reins wet and slack in my inexperienced hands.
I kicked the grey mare's sides
too hard and she moved into a canter
and my eyes shut tight against the cold morning fog.

I can hear my hostess putting the family silver
back in its satin-lined drawer. It seemed
sacrilegious to eat with these heirlooms
so we said grace before pulling the napkins
from their heavy rings. The linen
floated down onto our laps, a dumping ground
for stray scraps of chicken, dribbles of gravy and wine.
Brandy tumbled in a golden arc: the bananas
were melting crescent moons, grinning up
from their river of fire. In summer we rowed
like Olympians round the artificial loch
where the sun and the water clashed like glasses.
We cooled down then in the summer-house
reading aloud the signatures gouged into the rotting wood,
looping and spiralling against the grain
but still legible even after seven decades.

It will be very cold in my old-fashioned bedroom
surrounded by the dark, masculine furniture,
the free-standing full-length mirror
where I will laugh at myself wrapped in my many layers,
the grey woollen socks pulled up over my knees.
After the nervous laughter is out of my system
I will search the glass for another reflection
and whisper my prayers while still on my feet.
My soul is very drunk but respectful.
I will pull the blankets up over my head
shutting the world out. I will fear no evil.

The Sun Slips Over

The night floats outside my window,
a stray pale petal from a bouquet
or a butterfly to be netted
and pinned beneath glass in a case.
I see torn images in the clouds,
wings broken, weakly beating,
dying swans, each and every one.
Pavlova curves her graceful neck
into the feathered breast
of evening grass. The ribbon
unravels from slender ankles.
The sun slips over. Her mind
was still pirouetting, foot perfect
outside of her: she wanted to dance
but the cold overcame her.

Brief Encounter

Before the door slides open
I imagine here we are always
on the perimeter of shadow,
a city, its rock-propped castle.
You wait on the platform hunched
like a gargoyle in the cold stone.

The angle of the light was perfect
at the curve of coast where the rails
almost tipped us into the cold, blue Firth.
The landscape unclenched, my face and hair warmed.
I could have believed, just then,
that my life was charmed.

Your hair winds through my fingers.
My heart mimics the relentless engine
of your heart. Your body has a stoked-up heat
that even the light lacked.
We are setting our faces

against the dark but all I have
is a badly sketched skyline,
dipping and jutting, out of alignment.
I won't be telling you when I fall:
tonight you will think I am made of stone.

Pat Taffe and Arkle

Taffe was understandably amused by attempts to compare any
latter-day chasers with Arkle. He was adamant that there would
never be another horse like the Duchess of Westminster's champion.
TONY O'HEHIR, 1992

After the last exhausted horse
has stumbled past the winning-post
at Gowran Park, Dundalk and Fairyhouse
and the determined wind has uprooted
paper scraps and the thin covering of grass,
there is nowhere left for the eye to wander
beneath the black sky and the yellow stars.
The night carries your racing colours.

In the straw-strewn, cobbled stable-yard,
I am ringed by the bright nervous eyes
of the horses. I gather up the reins,
the leather cold and scuffed,
and settle myself into the creaking saddle.
Your ears are pricked, your eyes stare
straight ahead. If the truth be told
I had never quite come back to earth.

Marilyn Climbs Out of the Pool

He made her do the same scene
fifty times. Flashbulbs
light up her face
as she slips in and out
of the water with barely
a wrinkle of blue.

The cameras light up the pool
like bursts of applause.
Again and again she smiles
making hard work of it all,
bringing one glistening limb
right out of the water.
Her toes reach for the concrete edge:
her fair hair curls damply
over one bare shoulder.
Her eyes are the colour of the water,
night blue with silver
darting frantically in every direction.

On Location

A night of heavy rain and force eight winds:
the stars are pried loose like nails from the sky
and the black canvas billows and flails.
He has a limitless budget for special effects.
The wind rises like a curtain on a Victorian town
that he has reconstructed entirely from memory.
The bridge itself was easy, and the train.
The extras are growing tired of this scene.

The melodrama is wearing thin. They want to be
cowboys or Indians under blue skies and a hot sun.
On the neighbouring lot, a stentorian voice yells *Cut*
as the iceberg sinks before the ship.

Indian Summer

That summer was hotter than any other
in my life-time. My bare knees
itched and burned in the sand
as I dug and dug for the rusted coins
that Nanny had hidden that morning.
I'd watched her from my bedroom window.

The rugs hung heavy on the line
with a row of scalps put there to dry –
my whole family wiped out by Indians,
shock woven brightly into their faces.

The sky burned blue as a flame.
Grass browned. I could have rubbed
two stones together and the flare
would have shot me like a rocket
into the wilderness.

I exchanged the coins for a pony
the colour of gun-metal
and hoisted myself up into the saddle,
wincing as my half-peeled thighs
stuck to the hot leather,
and punctured his flanks with my spurs.
He hollered, balancing on his shaggy hind legs
before hitting the dirt at a gallop.

He stretched out over the blazing pampas
leaving my mother lying awkwardly
in the gaudily striped deck-chair,
blood dripping delicately
down the cut stem of her neck.

The Understudy

I bought a lipstick in a silver case;
understated, almost plain.
I gripped it in my hand:
my palm moulded to its simple lines
and I was a bright-eyed magician
holding a glittering wand
over the orphan Cinderella
waiting open-mouthed to be transformed.
I shrugged her off, became attuned
to Gloria Grahame, gravel-voiced
in the fifties: an edgy gangster's moll
jerking her head back
from the scalding spray.
I winced at her pain
and torched my own quivering mouth:
the wound stretched from corner to corner.
I stepped back from the harshly lit mirror,
all translucent skin and dark smudges,
lips swollen and ruby red.
I clicked my tongue and tossed my head
not taking my eyes from the sullen slut
whose unsteady hand moved out of frame
reaching for the coffee-pot.

The Dungeon

Only two of us managed it –
squeezing through the narrow
window-slit in the castle wall.
My skinny frame made it through
and no more, my face grazing
against grey brick. Outside
I could hear three anxious voices
and see the centre panel of a face
pinched into the breach;
a nose, one sky-blue eye. Their voices
receded as we slithered
over rocks and moss
plunging shakily into the murk,
the stuff of story books,
but minus the doubloons, the faded map
and the convenient escape route.

The Nightmare of the Gallops Watcher

An ocean cracks against the rocks.
The thoroughbred's nostrils flare
wide and red: her taut flanks
sweat as the spray breaks
in an arc as if from the broken neck
of a vast bottle. Light ricochets
from the glass: the gallops watcher,
up before dawn, his back
pressed against stone
watches the black mare
stride out over the sand.
Foam flecks white
over black muscle:
he lowers his binoculars.
His pencil moves quickly over paper.
The anonymous works rider spins her around.

He thinks he sees flame,
not sand, flying
from each glittering
bullet of a hoof
as the beast
bears down: caught
between cliff and horse
he spreads out his arms
and screams to shut out
the sound of splintering bone
as his face mashes into the pillow.

Playing the Clown

All these times she was away, a washed-out rag doll
in a hospital bed, you could have played with me.
We could have strolled along the beach together
kicking up the sand. I could have rolled my jeans up
above the shining pearl of my ankle bone
and splashed through the water, shrieking
at the cold, watching the waves form fluid arches
and collapse like ruined cities at our feet.
So it was only a dream. I'd have played the clown
and we'd have toppled together on the sand,
me giggling, you shouting your displeasure
as we rolled over, but given time, I'd have kissed
away your anger. You wouldn't have missed her.
We could have slept, curled up like dogs
in the great big bed. The man in black
could have walked to his heart's content
back and forward in front of the window all night.
You'd have plucked the screams like cherries
from my mouth, as I feigned sleep.
I could have been anything if you'd only let me.

Big Girls

Granny's here. Her mother's voice was bright
with pleasure. She turned away in spite.
Hello, she mumbled and dropped her eyes back
to the book she was reading. It was a book
for Big Girls. The knowledge stuffed her
with pride. Granny could go to Hell:
she slept on an unsightly brown and orange
floral camp bed in her bedroom
and snored and littered her face creams
all over the spotless dressing table,
but when she left she gave her money
and then she smiled. *Have a pleasant journey home.*
Choosing could take all morning, but it was fun:
Endless Night, The Mirror Crack'd,
Cat Among the Pigeons, Sparkling Cyanide.

After the Impossible Dream

Rubbing sleep from her eyes, cradling
twigs for the fire, she saw a mouse
scampering across the floor.
It ran around the grate
and turned to face her
sitting up on its two hind legs,
big as a mastiff,
its teeth straight and white
as a beauty queen's.
When Cinderella blinked
and looked again

the mouse had vanished
and on the mantelpiece
she spotted an ornament
she couldn't remember
ever having dusted.
It was her little world
in a glass bubble.
My glass slipper, she cried
and the flames in the grate leapt up
in a heavenly chorus.
She took the glass lovingly
in her scarred hands

and hurled it to the floor:
Cinderella, leaning over
her shattered portrait,
picked up a handful of glass
and nibbled the shards
as if they were cheese
and she the mouse that had drawn the carriage
before it turned into a monster.

She rubbed the flesh ragged
from her wrists, laughing delightedly:
a young girl
waltzing with her Prince.

Her open veins shone, emeralds
awash in a sea of rubies;
her body no longer battered
but a jewel, Cinderella having played
the glass slipper game
to the very end.

The Front-Runner

The horses swing round: each well-
muscled, half a ton of flesh
crushing the grass stalks down.
Their hooves spit stones,
enticed by the whip and the crowd's
dark roar. Dig down

beyond the chest's thick bone
and damp, coarse hair.
Dig down. The black runner
pitches over in a blur
of stick and brush,
his flailing finish premature:

the bursting heart, bright
as silks, fluttering briefly
as his rivals take repeated flight.

The Exhibits

In the museum of translucent
blue skins, the exhibits lie
soaking up the darkness, flat
as pricked balloons.

The girl with the bruised eyes
was unzipped from black plastic
and laid out
so that her parents could identify
what was no longer anybody's daughter.

The Bully

She was a fat, white doll,
too heavy to cradle
but always ready
with a smile or a sob.
In summer, how she sweated.
I prayed she might melt
like ice cream or lard:
she could barely run
but trickled down the road.
One afternoon, on the way home
from school, she dripped
over a gate, demanding money.
My hand twitched:

I grabbed the violent darling's hair,
bell-ringer to her screams.
When her curls disentangled
from my fingers, she ran off
blubbering down the dusty road.
I couldn't quite feel pleased
but the summer sun
and my brief, painless exertion
lightened my mood.

Sleepless

The water blinked my white face back at me.
Yours tossed and turned beside it, our two heads
restless on one starry pillow, our eyes raised
skywards. The stars said it was meant to be.
I performed my simple ceremony.

One small act: twisting till my finger hurt,
I cast my gold band out after our drowned
images and watched as it was lost
under the bridge, a perfect suicide
plunging down through circles of ghosts.

Gia

In drugstores across America
on laminated cards at points-of-sale
her lips are the glistening focus,
freshly painted with Melon-Shine,
the season's new shade from Maybelline.
In magazines, she struggles against a fake storm
with an umbrella by Christian Dior.

New York: a seventies summer.
A small apartment, spartanly furnished.
The morning is already warm,
the windows flung wide open
to catch the sun's first sweet rush
before the sidewalks bake and crack.
On the cover of August's *Vogue*
the model's complexion is as flawless
as a fresh snowfall
and her eyes are open very wide
in a halo of mink and klieg lights.

Southampton, Long Island: a week-long shoot.
Her chestnut hair is piled high on her head.
She rests her bare feet on a rock
and her hands paddle in the sparkling blue water.
The tide slaps against the track-marks
that run from wrist to elbow.

She is prowling in a thin black dress
on the roof of a building two hundred feet up
in the heart of the garment district:
black stockings, heels, slant eyes, a scowl.
A freezing wind sways the building.

In the darkroom the pictures float
in their tray of developing-fluid.
The emerging face is defiant and sad.
The eyes are dead, the fabulous body
is stripped of its flesh.
He lifts out the bones of the drowned girl.

On the Glittering Beaches

Growing tired of her hysterical gestures,
the way she wheeled and soared like a gull
round the cramped front room of their house,
he withdrew his presence, subtly at first:
a minute's silence when one word
was called for, a phone-call forgotten,
an eyebrow raised instead of an answer.

He turned his back when he came to bed,
later and later, ignoring the feeble creature
in one corner who'd smashed all her eggs
on the bare mattress springs and smeared
the spidery foetuses over her flesh.
She called to him from a great distance
as if searching the glittering beaches
of sleep in vain, for her mate.

Hyperion's Bones

In a garden shed two tea-chests
gave their treasure protection
from the light and whipping draughts.

No ordinary bones, the caption
reads, beneath the intricate
resurrection of your skeleton:

once *a glowing chestnut with four white
fetlocks*, barely larger than a pony,
but *deep through the chest*,

who swept past giants to win his Derby
and was named for a god.
There is something lacking in the rigid display:

the carriage of that handsome head
is stiff, not *extraordinarily proud*.
Common sense says the spirit's fled

the tea-chests and the garden shed
sneezed out from its dusty bones.
On a windswept Heath, the ghosts are on parade.

All May, the rain's drummed down
loud as hoofbeats on your old training ground.
The weather clears in June.

The final furlong sees the sun strike gold,
distancing itself with contemptuous ease
from the chasing pack of black clouds.

Artifice

It was no wild landscape, merely
a frost-pinched narrow lane
making its deliberate way
between fields and the back
walls of gardens, the sun
set at its mid-morning slant.
Primly it sat like an ornament
on its dustless mantelpiece, or
a photograph of a mirthless
child. Everything seemed
to be exactly where it should.
I added little flowers of detail
plucked from hidden childhood places:
a mother stiffly pushing an antique
navy-covered pram, on her way home
from coffee with a friend.
She stoops briefly to stroke
a ginger-tom, streaked
with more lively shades
of sun. Baby is silent,
patting a stuffed monkey
on her pillow, sweating under
her layers of wool. The only sounds
are the wheels bumping
over hard-packed dirt and the cat
back on his wall, purring
warmly enough to melt the frost.
He soon lost interest
in the pair as they trundled
out of focus, into a colder,
less assured picture, into
the deep, dark woods, those beloved
of fairytales.

NO HIDING PLACE

I rode down to the street floor and went out on the steps of the City Hall. It was a cool day and very clear. You could see a long way – but not as far as Velma had gone.

RAYMOND CHANDLER: *Farewell, My Lovely*

Outside the bathroom door
and half a world away I hear her scream
and hurl a hairbrush at the mirror
that dares to show the passage of time
on her once beautiful face, before floating
mine across the glass to take its place.

*   *   *

The water is fragrant with winter
and is the colour of holly-berries.
The steam slides upwards from each shin.
I am shedding you both like a skin.

I will find it as if by accident,
the dilapidated warehouse squatting
over a hot sewage-plugged river. The last hours
will be a blank, my clothes filthy and torn
and the gun heavy in my hands.
The bodies will float gently over to me
although there is no motion at all
to the water and I will bend down
and their faces will be familiar.

                    *   *   *

I always knew that one day
they would come for me:
last night the phone jangled
into my dreams and my hand jerked out.
I mumbled my name and the line went dead.

We were on holiday
in the Lake District.
I was ten. One morning
on the kitchen linoleum, I saw
a stack of old newspapers
ready for collection.
On the front page of one of them
a woman sat, cross-legged and burning
in a busy London park.
I looked closer. Her face
was stretched taut, her hair
was a forest alight at its scraggy edges
and in the distance, the charcoal
figure of a policeman was frozen
into his stride.

We took a rowing boat out
on Lake Windermere. It was
a real Indian summer.
Dad took the oars as we crossed the lake.
She sat in the middle of the water.
I asked dad for a better word for blaze:
he suggested *conflagration*.
She bobbed a little closer,
conflagrant and brazen.

Her face was pulp; one eye
slid down her cheek like a cracked egg.
I showed her her reflection
just before she died. I thought
it would be appropriate,
the two of us together
staring the mirror down.

He lay beside her, his mouth
half-open in protest:
inside his pocket
a scribbled address
inside a match-book
bearing the legend *Loser*
and a crumpled betting slip.

It was a desperate close finish,
no more than half a head in it
as they crossed the line.
Turn the Other Cheek
was just shaded by *Revenge*:
there were no excuses for the rags.
It was a fine late run.

Her closed fist hammering on my door;
an open window, the wobbling drainpipe
leading down into the dark, the stars
twitching overhead, my feet
touching the tarmac just before the door fell in
and I was sprinting up the driveway
to the street, past the neighbour's garden
where I'd lost a thousand tennis balls,
my lousy backhand sending them
wildly over the high hedge.
I could still hear them bounce
over the imaginary lines drawn in the street,
my best friend's triumphant screech of *Out!*

Only at the threshold of death
are we truly alive. At last.

I am aware of my erratic heartbeat
and her silence.

All her life she spent, stiff and white
as laundry pinned on a frozen line.

But there are limits to my sympathies.
I stand ankle-deep in the evidence.

All the blood. Her wash-day skills,
the immaculate row of sheets,

her thin, raw fingers darting like snakes
in the drum of the washing machine.

Life was unkind to her she often said
but she left her mark,

the scarlet petals that flared up
on the soft skin at the back of my thighs.

All the blood mother. The bloody handprints.
Wash them out.

I stand in what used to be
my bedroom: thin strips
of candy pink wallpaper
are running like tears
down the grey walls.
The room is freezing
even in summer; the sun
stopped dead at the glass.
This was a cold house.

*   *   *

He rarely ventured out.
She locked him up
in their daughter's old bedroom
with a blunt pair of scissors
where he would sit for hours
cutting out ragged chains
of newspaper dolls.
He unfolded them around him
in a fairy ring.

*   *   *

A girl sits in a cold bedroom.
The garish curtains are slightly parted,
a book lies open on the sill.
She is only two–dimensional.

be it ever so humble

Grandmother, your hands are ice,
each finger a bruised and frozen lake.
Beneath our feet the wooden porch-steps creak
like shifting continental plates.
Your face dissolves in hail and sleet.

My spinster aunt, your eldest girl
who died in a house-fire
in her fortieth year,
pours us tea then disappears.
Your father never visits me.
You take up the old refrain
as if it was knitting you'd laid aside,
saving it for the cold nights.
My only son, your voice clacks on,
he crawls behind your mother
like a worm, his soft belly
sinking into the carpet
at her feet.
She clears her throat of earth
and small stones.
No wonder you're queer, child.

Even though the afternoon is dark
the lights I flick on
are snuffed out by my parsimonious aunt
and the moon has the pinched beam
of a pocket torch.

*   *   *

They are gracious, smiling through their tears
like young lovers. He compliments her
on her blue, old-fashioned dress:
it brings out the colour of your eyes...
you are just as lovely as when we first met...

I am sitting in the back garden
with a book: *Nancy Drew and the Clue
in the Crumbling Wall.*
The sun has stained the pages yellow
making my cheap paperback
almost a museum-piece
and now makes me squint but reluctant
to raise my eyes or move
even when the cold
starts to slide like water
over my ankles and my mother
shouts from the house
This is your last chance.

*   *   *

I am sitting on the green tiles
of a swimming pool
still holding my book.
The print is huge.
The water is over my head
and the sun is minute,
floating just out of my reach.
The story is gripping
and there are only a few pages left.
If I force myself to read very slowly
I can make it last for another lifetime
and still be out of the water
before it gets completely dark.